# KIDS

## Coloring book

## FOR

## Boy & Girl

## RELAXATION

## 4-8 YEARS

# This book belong to

___________________________

___________________________

hungry

fast

# cute

# calm

energetic

# mischievous

# ashamed

# tired

sleepy

cheerful

# clean

# smart

honest

funny

comfortable

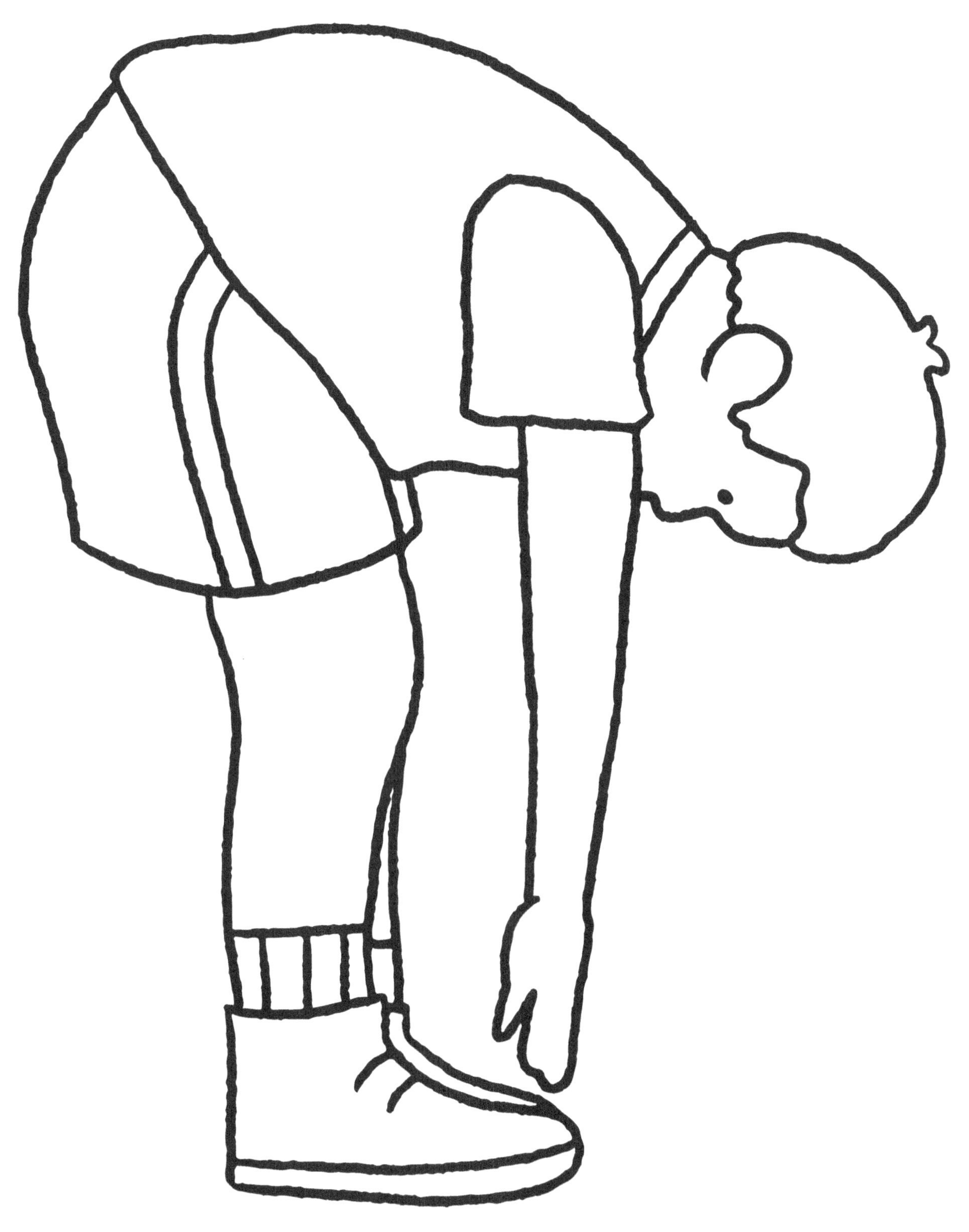

grumpy

upset

# brave

# anxious

quiet

SLEEP

# WATER

# EAT

THINK

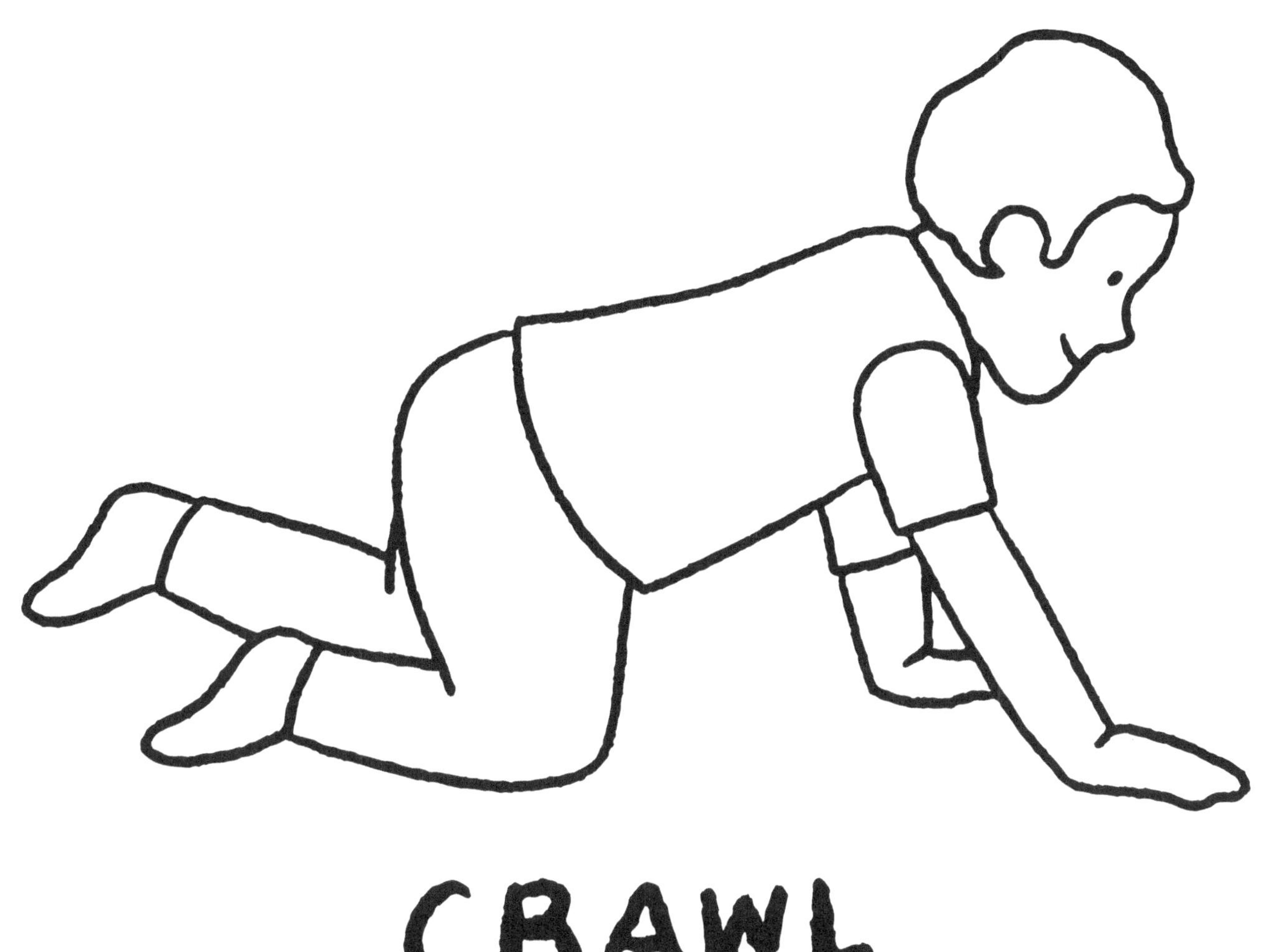

# CRAWL

# DRINK

yusuf's Designs

# PULL

yusuf's Designs

# THROW

LIFT

SIT

# PLAY

# PAINT

# READ

CRY

# excited

# dirty

loud

# romantic

aggressive

# dizzy